History of Papacy

A comprehensive guide to the epic
story of the Catholic Church's
highest office

James Burke

Table of Contents

Introduction

The Papacy, the highest office of the Catholic Church, has stood as a formidable and enduring institution for nearly two millennia. From its humble beginnings with Saint Peter, traditionally regarded as the first Pope, to its current incarnation under Pope Francis, the Papacy has wielded immense spiritual, political, and cultural influence. This profound impact extends far beyond the confines of the Church, shaping the course of world history and playing a pivotal role in major global events and movements.

The significance of the Papacy lies in its dual role: spiritual leadership and temporal power. As the spiritual leader of over a billion Catholics worldwide, the Pope serves as a shepherd guiding the faithful in matters of doctrine, morality, and worship. This role is not merely symbolic but carries real authority and responsibility, influencing the beliefs and practices of millions. Beyond the religious sphere, the Papacy has often been a key political player. Throughout the Middle Ages, Popes crowned emperors, negotiated peace treaties, and wielded significant influence over European monarchs. Even today, the Vatican, the seat of the Papacy, acts as a sovereign entity engaging in international diplomacy.

This book, "History of Papacy: A Comprehensive Guide to the Epic Story of the Catholic Church's Highest Office," aims to provide an extensive and nuanced exploration of the Papacy's rich and complex history. Our journey begins in the early Christian period, tracing the origins and evolution of the Papal office. We will explore the transformative moments and key figures that have defined the Papacy, from the consolidation of papal authority in the early Middle Ages to the profound reforms of the Renaissance Popes, and the challenges of the modern era.

The book is organized chronologically, with each chapter dedicated to a significant era in

Papal history. This structure allows readers to follow the development of the Papacy in a linear fashion, understanding how each period built upon its predecessor. We will delve into the lives and legacies of notable Popes, examining their contributions and controversies. Special attention is given to the context in which these Popes operated, providing insights into the broader historical, cultural, and political landscapes of their times.

Our approach combines rigorous historical scholarship with accessible storytelling. We have drawn on a wealth of primary and secondary sources, offering a balanced and comprehensive perspective. Detailed analyses of significant events, such as the Great Schism, the Reformation, and the Second Vatican Council, are presented alongside intriguing anecdotes and lesser-known episodes that bring the narrative to life.

Ultimately, this book seeks to illuminate the multifaceted nature of the Papacy, an institution that has not only shaped the Catholic Church but has also left an indelible mark on world history. Whether you are a scholar, a devout Catholic, or a curious reader, we invite you to embark on this journey through the centuries, discovering the epic story of the Catholic Church's highest office.

Part 1: The Early Papacy (33 AD - 500 AD)

Chapter 1: The Apostolic Era (33 AD - 100 AD)

The Life and Legacy of Saint Peter and the Early Christian Community

The story of the Papacy begins with Saint Peter, one of Jesus Christ's twelve apostles and the man traditionally recognized as the first Pope. According to the Gospels, Jesus bestowed a special role upon Peter, symbolized by the metaphor of the "rock" upon which Christ would build his Church (Matthew 16:18). After Christ's crucifixion and resurrection, Peter emerged as a central figure among the early Christians, playing a crucial role in spreading the new faith.

Peter's missionary journeys, including his foundational work in Rome, are seminal to understanding the early Papacy. Arriving in the imperial capital, Peter helped establish the Christian community there, enduring persecution under Emperor Nero and ultimately facing martyrdom around 64 AD. His leadership and sacrifice left an indelible mark on the fledgling Church, cementing his legacy as the cornerstone of the Papal tradition.

The early Christian community, though small and often persecuted, was dynamic and diverse. Composed of both Jewish and Gentile converts, these early Christians faced significant challenges, from external threats of persecution to internal theological disputes. Despite these challenges, they remained steadfast, guided by a sense of mission and the teachings of the apostles, especially Peter. His leadership helped maintain unity and doctrinal integrity, setting precedents for the role and authority of future Popes.

The Development of the Papacy's Role and Authority

In its nascent stages, the Papacy's authority was more implied than formally defined. Peter's prominence among the apostles laid the groundwork for the Roman bishop's primacy, but the organizational structure of the early Church was still evolving. Bishops in various cities, including Antioch, Alexandria, and Jerusalem, held significant sway in their regions, yet Rome gradually began to assume a special status.

This period saw the formation of key doctrines and the establishment of ecclesiastical hierarchies. Letters and epistles from early Christian leaders, such as the Pauline Epistles, reflect the emerging structures and roles within the Church. As the Christian faith spread throughout the Roman Empire, the need for a central, authoritative voice became apparent. The bishops of Rome, successors of Saint Peter, naturally filled this role, drawing on the apostle's legacy to assert their spiritual authority.

Chapter 2: The Patristic Era (100 AD - 500 AD)

The Papacy's Growth and Influence During the Early Christian Centuries

The second chapter of Papal history encompasses the Patristic Era, a period marked by significant theological development and consolidation of Church authority. As Christianity grew from a persecuted sect into a major religious force within the Roman Empire, the role of the Papacy expanded accordingly. Bishops of Rome began to play an increasingly prominent role in addressing theological disputes and guiding the broader Christian community.

This era saw the Papacy involved in major controversies and heresies, such as Gnosticism and Arianism, which threatened the unity of the Church. The Roman bishops, drawing on their connection to Peter, asserted their authority in theological debates, helping to shape orthodox doctrine. The Council of Nicaea in 325 AD, convened by Emperor Constantine, was a pivotal moment in this regard. While the bishop of Rome did not attend, his legates did, reinforcing Rome's growing influence.

The legalization of Christianity under Constantine and its eventual establishment as the state religion under Theodosius I profoundly impacted the Papacy. With the Christianization of the Roman Empire, the bishops of Rome found themselves at the intersection of spiritual and temporal power, setting the stage for the Papacy's future political role.

Key Figures: Saint Irenaeus, Saint Cyprian, and Saint Augustine

Several key figures during this era played crucial roles in the development of the Papacy and Christian doctrine. Saint Irenaeus of Lyons (c. 130 – c. 202) was instrumental in combating Gnosticism and emphasizing the importance of apostolic succession. His works, especially "Against Heresies," underscored the authority of the bishops, particularly the bishop of Rome, in maintaining doctrinal purity.

Saint Cyprian of Carthage (c. 200 – 258) further developed the concept of ecclesiastical unity under a single, authoritative Church. His famous assertion, "There is no salvation outside the Church," highlighted the importance of communion with the bishop of Rome. During times of persecution and internal strife, Cyprian's writings reinforced the central role of the Papacy in ensuring the unity and integrity of the Christian faith.

Saint Augustine of Hippo (354 – 430), one of the most influential theologians in Christian history, also played a significant role in shaping early Church doctrine. His extensive writings on grace, free will, and the nature of the Church contributed to the theological foundation upon which later Popes would build. Augustine's acknowledgment of the authority of the Roman see further solidified the Papacy's central role in the Western Church.

By the end of the Patristic Era, the Papacy had firmly established itself as the spiritual leader of Western Christianity. The groundwork laid by these early figures and the theological developments of the period set the stage for the medieval Papacy's ascent to unprecedented influence and authority. As we move forward in this comprehensive guide, we will see how the seeds planted during these formative centuries blossomed into one of the most powerful institutions in world history.

Part 2: The Middle Ages (500 AD - 1500 AD)

Chapter 3: The Byzantine Era (500 AD - 800 AD)

The Papacy's Relationship with the Eastern Roman Empire and the Rise of Monasticism

The Middle Ages began with the Papacy deeply intertwined with the Eastern Roman Empire, also known as the Byzantine Empire. This period was marked by a complex and often contentious relationship between the Papacy and the Byzantine emperors, who exerted significant influence over the Church. Despite being geographically distant from the imperial court in Constantinople, the Popes of Rome navigated a delicate balance of asserting ecclesiastical independence while maintaining political alliances.

One of the key developments during this era was the rise of monasticism, which profoundly shaped the spiritual and administrative life of the Church. Monastic communities, following the Rule of Saint Benedict, became centers of learning, piety, and missionary work. These communities provided a stabilizing force during times of political turmoil and played a crucial role in preserving classical knowledge and Christian teachings.

Key Figures: Saint Gregory the Great and Charlemagne

Saint Gregory the Great (c. 540 – 604), one of the most influential Popes of this era, significantly redefined the Papacy. Elected in 590, Gregory faced a Rome besieged by plague, famine, and barbarian threats. His pragmatic leadership and administrative reforms earned him the title "Great." Gregory strengthened papal authority, reformed the liturgy, and dispatched missionaries, such as Augustine of

Canterbury, to convert the Anglo-Saxons. His writings, particularly the "Pastoral Rule," set enduring standards for episcopal conduct.

The Papacy's relationship with the Frankish kingdom marked a turning point in this era, culminating in the alliance with Charlemagne (c. 742 – 814). On Christmas Day in 800 AD, Pope Leo III crowned Charlemagne as Emperor of the Romans, effectively reviving the Western Roman Empire. This act established the precedent for the Holy Roman Empire and solidified the Pope's role as a kingmaker, intertwining the destinies of the Papacy and Western European monarchs.

Chapter 4: The High Middle Ages (800 AD - 1300 AD)

The Papacy's Centralization of Power and the Rise of the Holy Roman Empire

The High Middle Ages witnessed the Papacy consolidating its spiritual and temporal power. This period saw the Papacy asserting dominance over secular rulers and centralizing Church governance. The reforms initiated during the Gregorian Reform movement (named after Pope Gregory VII) sought to eliminate simony, enforce clerical celibacy, and assert the Church's independence from secular influence.

The Investiture Controversy, a major conflict between Pope Gregory VII and Emperor Henry IV over the appointment of bishops, epitomized the struggle between the Papacy and secular authorities. The resolution of this conflict, through the Concordat of Worms in 1122, established the principle of papal supremacy in ecclesiastical appointments.

Key Figures: Innocent III and Boniface VIII

Pope Innocent III (1161 – 1216) epitomized the apex of papal power during the High Middle Ages. His pontificate (1198-1216) marked a period of significant political and spiritual authority. Innocent III not only asserted control over secular rulers but also initiated the Fourth Crusade and convened the Fourth Lateran Council in 1215, which enacted numerous Church reforms and defined key doctrines.

Boniface VIII (c. 1230 – 1303), though his reign was marked by conflict, further demonstrated the Papacy's ambition to wield temporal power. His issuance of the papal bull "Unam Sanctam" in 1302 declared the necessity of submission to the Pope for salvation, reflecting the height of papal claims to authority. However, his confrontations with King Philip IV of France exposed the limits of papal power and foreshadowed future conflicts.

Chapter 5: The Late Middle Ages (1300 AD - 1500 AD)

The Papacy's Challenges During the Avignon Papacy and the Western Schism

The Late Middle Ages brought significant challenges to the Papacy, beginning with the Avignon Papacy (1309-1377), a period when the Popes resided in Avignon, France, rather than Rome. This relocation, influenced by political pressures from the French crown, led to perceptions of the Papacy as being under French control, weakening its universal authority.

The subsequent Western Schism (1378-1417), wherein multiple claimants to the Papal throne emerged, further fractured the Church. This schism eroded the Papacy's credibility and divided Christendom. Efforts to resolve the schism culminated in the Council of Constance (1414-1418), which ended the schism by deposing the rival Popes and electing Martin V, restoring unity to the Church.

Key Figures: Catherine of Siena and the Council of Constance

Catherine of Siena (1347-1380), a mystic and reformer, played a crucial role during the Avignon Papacy. Her fervent letters to Pope Gregory XI urging him to return to Rome exemplified her influence. Canonized in 1461, Catherine's commitment to Church reform and her deep spirituality left a lasting impact on the Papacy and Catholic piety.

The Council of Constance was pivotal in resolving the Western Schism and addressing calls for reform within the Church. It asserted conciliar authority over papal authority in certain instances, a principle that had enduring implications for Church governance. The council also condemned Jan Hus, a precursor to later reformers, highlighting the growing tensions that would eventually lead to the Reformation.

By the end of the Middle Ages, the Papacy had weathered significant trials and transformations. These centuries saw the Papacy evolve from a position of precarious authority within the Byzantine Empire to a central and sometimes contested role in European politics. As we move forward, we will explore how the Papacy navigated the profound changes of the Renaissance and Reformation, shaping the modern era.

Part 3: The Renaissance and Reformation (1500 AD - 1700 AD)

Chapter 6: The Renaissance Papacy (1500 AD - 1550 AD)

The Papacy's Cultural and Artistic Achievements During the Renaissance

The Renaissance was a period of extraordinary cultural and artistic flourishing, and the Papacy played a pivotal role in this revival. The Renaissance Papacy, centered in Rome, became a patron of the arts, commissioning some of the most renowned works in Western history. This era saw the construction and decoration of iconic buildings such as St. Peter's Basilica and the Sistine Chapel, transforming Rome into a vibrant center of Renaissance culture.

Popes like Julius II and Leo X were instrumental in this transformation. Julius II, known as the "Warrior Pope," not only sought to extend the temporal power of the Papacy but also initiated ambitious artistic projects. He commissioned Michelangelo to paint the Sistine Chapel ceiling and Raphael to decorate the Vatican Stanze, creating masterpieces that continue to draw admiration today.

Leo X, a member of the influential Medici family, continued Julius II's patronage of the arts. Under his papacy, Rome saw the flourishing of Renaissance humanism, with the Papal court becoming a hub for artists, scholars, and poets. Leo X's reign, however, was also marked by financial extravagance, which would have long-term consequences for the Church.

Key Figures: Leo X and Clement VII

Pope Leo X (1475-1521), elected in 1513, epitomized the Renaissance Papacy's blend of cultural patronage and political ambition. His support for the arts was unparalleled, fostering the careers of artists like Raphael and funding grand architectural projects. However, Leo X's financial mismanagement, including the sale of indulgences, contributed to growing discontent that would soon erupt into the Protestant Reformation.

Clement VII (1478-1534), a cousin of Leo X, faced the turbulent aftermath of these developments. His papacy (1523-1534) was marked by significant political and military challenges, including the sack of Rome in 1527 by the troops of Emperor Charles V. This event symbolized the declining political power of the Papacy and underscored the urgent need for reform within the Church. Clement VII's inability to effectively address the growing Protestant threat further highlighted the vulnerabilities of the Renaissance Papacy.

Chapter 7: The Reformation and Counter-Reformation (1550 AD - 1700 AD)

The Papacy's Response to the Protestant Reformation and the Rise of the Jesuits

The Protestant Reformation, initiated by Martin Luther in 1517, posed the most significant challenge to the Papacy in centuries. The Reformation rapidly spread across Europe, leading to the fragmentation of Christendom and the establishment of Protestant churches independent of papal authority. The Papacy's response, known as the Counter-Reformation, aimed to address the criticisms raised by reformers and to revitalize the Catholic Church.

Central to the Counter-Reformation was the Council of Trent (1545-1563), which played a crucial role in defining Catholic doctrine and reforming Church practices. The council addressed issues such as clerical corruption, the sale of indulgences, and the need for improved clerical education. It reaffirmed core Catholic doctrines, including the sacraments and the authority of the Pope, and established measures to improve discipline and piety within the Church.

The rise of new religious orders, particularly the Society of Jesus (Jesuits) founded by Ignatius of Loyola, was instrumental in the Counter-Reformation. The Jesuits became the Papacy's most effective agents in combating Protestantism, focusing on education, missionary work, and the revitalization of Catholic spirituality. Their influence extended across Europe and into the New World, making significant contributions to Catholic renewal.

Key Figures: Pius V and Innocent X

Pope Pius V (1504-1572), who reigned from 1566 to 1572, was a central figure in the Counter-Reformation. Known for his piety and austerity, Pius V implemented the decrees of the

Council of Trent with vigor. He standardized the Mass with the Roman Missal of 1570 and reformed the administration of the Papal States. Pius V also formed the Holy League, which achieved a decisive victory against the Ottoman Empire at the Battle of Lepanto in 1571, reinforcing the Papacy's role as a defender of Christendom.

Pope Innocent X (1574-1655), who reigned from 1644 to 1655, led the Church during a time of continued religious and political upheaval. His papacy is notable for the conclusion of the Thirty Years' War, a conflict that devastated much of Europe and had profound religious implications. The Peace of Westphalia in 1648, which ended the war, marked a significant shift in the political landscape, with the recognition of the independence of Protestant states. Innocent X's efforts to oppose certain terms of the peace, particularly those that limited papal influence, highlighted the continuing struggle for power and authority in a changing world.

The Renaissance and Reformation were transformative periods for the Papacy, marked by both grand achievements and profound challenges. The cultural and artistic legacy of the Renaissance Papacy continues to be celebrated, while the reforms of the Counter-Reformation helped to renew and strengthen the Catholic Church. As we move into the modern era, the Papacy would continue to navigate the complexities of a rapidly changing world, adapting and evolving in response to new challenges and opportunities.

Part 4: The Modern Era (1700 AD - present)

Chapter 8: The Enlightenment and the French Revolution (1700 AD - 1800 AD)

The Papacy's Challenges During the Enlightenment and the French Revolution

The Enlightenment, an intellectual movement emphasizing reason, science, and secularism, posed significant challenges to the Papacy in the 18th century. Enlightenment thinkers often criticized the Church's influence and dogma, advocating for religious tolerance, separation of church and state, and individual liberty. These ideas undermined the traditional authority of the Papacy and prompted widespread secularization.

The French Revolution (1789-1799) brought these tensions to a head. Revolutionary leaders viewed the Catholic Church as an ally of the monarchy and an impediment to progress. Consequently, they enacted measures to curtail the Church's power, including the confiscation of Church property, the suppression of religious orders, and the imposition of the Civil Constitution of the Clergy, which aimed to bring the Church under state control. These actions led to widespread persecution of clergy and a rupture between the French state and the Papacy.

Key Figures: Pius VI and Pius VII

Pope Pius VI (1717-1799), who reigned from 1775 to 1799, faced the brunt of these challenges. He condemned the principles of the Enlightenment and the revolutionary changes in France. Pius VI's opposition to the Civil Constitution of the Clergy led to his capture and exile by French revolutionary forces, highlighting the Papacy's vulnerability during this tumultuous period. He died in captivity in 1799, a symbol of the Church's struggle against revolutionary forces.

Pope Pius VII (1742-1823), who succeeded Pius VI, navigated the complex post-revolutionary landscape. Reigning from 1800 to 1823, Pius VII initially sought to reconcile with Napoleon Bonaparte, signing the Concordat of 1801, which restored some degree of religious freedom and property to the Church in France. However, tensions resurfaced as Napoleon sought to exert control over the Church. Pius VII's subsequent imprisonment by Napoleon from 1809 to 1814 underscored the ongoing conflict between secular authority and the Papacy. His resilience and eventual return to Rome symbolized the enduring strength of the Papal office.

Chapter 9: The 19th and 20th Centuries (1800 AD - 2000 AD)

The Papacy's Response to Modernism, Liberalism, and the Second Vatican Council

The 19th and 20th centuries brought new ideological challenges, including modernism and liberalism, which promoted scientific progress, individual rights, and secular governance. The Papacy responded to these challenges with a mixture of resistance and adaptation.

Pope Pius IX (1792-1878), who reigned from 1846 to 1878, exemplified the Papacy's initial resistance to modernist ideas. His Syllabus of Errors (1864) condemned numerous liberal and modernist propositions, and the First Vatican Council (1869-1870) defined the dogma of papal infallibility. However, Pius IX's loss of the Papal States in 1870, when Italian unification forces seized Rome, marked a significant reduction in the Papacy's temporal power.

The 20th century saw the Papacy increasingly engage with the modern world. Pope John XXIII (1881-1963), who reigned from 1958 to 1963, initiated the Second Vatican Council (1962-1965), a transformative event aimed at modernizing the Church. Vatican II addressed relations between the Church and the contemporary world, promoting ecumenism, revising the liturgy, and encouraging a more pastoral approach to ministry. These reforms sought to renew the Church's relevance in a rapidly changing society.

Pope John Paul II (1920-2005), who reigned from 1978 to 2005, further engaged with global issues, advocating for human rights, social justice, and interfaith dialogue. His extensive travels and charismatic presence revitalized the Papacy's global influence. John Paul II's role in opposing communism, particularly in his native Poland, highlighted the Papacy's continued political significance.

Chapter 10: The Contemporary Papacy (2000 AD - present)

The Papacy's Current Challenges and Opportunities in the Modern World

The 21st century presents the Papacy with both enduring and new challenges, including secularization, interfaith relations, and social issues. The Papacy continues to navigate the balance between upholding traditional doctrines and engaging with contemporary societal changes.

Pope Benedict XVI (1927-2022), who reigned from 2005 to 2013, faced the complex task of addressing the Church's internal crises, including the clerical sexual abuse scandal. His theological rigor and emphasis on traditional values sometimes contrasted with the demands of a modernizing world. Benedict XVI's unprecedented resignation in 2013 underscored the evolving nature of the Papal office in the contemporary era.

Pope Francis (1936-present), elected in 2013, has sought to address these challenges with a focus on pastoral care, humility, and social justice. His emphasis on issues such as climate change, economic inequality, and migrant rights reflects a commitment to addressing global concerns. Francis has also pursued greater transparency and reform within the Church, particularly in response to the sexual abuse crisis. His efforts to promote dialogue with other faiths and his progressive stance on social issues mark a significant shift in the Papacy's approach to modernity.

The contemporary Papacy, under Francis's leadership, continues to grapple with maintaining doctrinal integrity while engaging with an increasingly pluralistic and secular world. The Papacy's ability to adapt to these challenges will shape its role and influence in the years to come.

As we conclude this comprehensive guide to the history of the Papacy, we see a narrative of resilience, adaptation, and profound influence. From its early beginnings with Saint Peter to its current challenges under Pope Francis, the Papacy remains a central and enduring institution within the Catholic Church and the broader global community. The epic story of the Papacy is one of continual transformation, reflecting the dynamic interplay between faith, power, and the ever-changing tides of history.

Conclusion

The epic story of the Papacy is one of remarkable resilience, profound influence, and enduring impact on both the Catholic Church and the world. From its inception with Saint Peter, the Papacy has navigated the tumultuous waters of history, emerging as a symbol of spiritual authority and a beacon of faith for over a billion Catholics worldwide.

Throughout the centuries, the Papacy has played a pivotal role in shaping religious, political, and cultural landscapes. In the early days, the Apostolic Era saw the Papacy laying the foundations of the Christian community, with Saint Peter's legacy establishing a tradition of leadership and authority that would guide the Church through the ages. As the Church expanded during the Patristic Era, figures like Saint Augustine helped to solidify the theological and doctrinal foundations that continue to underpin Catholicism today.

The Middle Ages brought both challenges and triumphs. The Byzantine Era highlighted the Papacy's delicate balancing act with the Eastern Roman Empire, while the High Middle Ages saw the Papacy asserting its dominance over secular rulers and navigating the complexities of the Holy Roman Empire. The Late Middle Ages, marked by the Avignon Papacy and the Western Schism, tested the Papacy's unity and resilience, ultimately leading to significant reforms and a strengthened Church.

The Renaissance Papacy's patronage of the arts and culture left an indelible mark on history, transforming Rome into a center of artistic and intellectual brilliance. Yet, this period also set the stage for the Protestant Reformation, a seismic shift that challenged the very foundations of the Papal authority. The Counter-Reformation, led by determined Popes and the rise of new religious orders like the Jesuits, revitalized the Church and reaffirmed its spiritual mission.

In the Modern Era, the Papacy confronted the Enlightenment's secular challenges and navigated the upheaval of the French Revolution. The 19th and 20th centuries saw the Papacy responding to the tides of modernism and liberalism, with significant moments such as the First Vatican Council and the transformative Second Vatican Council reshaping the Church's engagement with the modern world. Leaders like Pius IX, John XXIII, and John Paul II guided the Church through these complex times, leaving lasting legacies of doctrinal clarity, ecumenical outreach, and global influence.

Today, the Papacy under Pope Francis faces new challenges and opportunities in an increasingly pluralistic and secular world. The contemporary Papacy continues to address pressing issues such as climate change, social justice, and interfaith dialogue, demonstrating the Papal office's ongoing relevance and adaptability.

Reflecting on the lessons and legacies of the Papacy's history, several key themes emerge. The Papacy's ability to adapt and respond to changing circumstances has been crucial to its enduring influence. Whether confronting heresies, political upheavals, or calls for reform, the Papacy has demonstrated a remarkable capacity for resilience and renewal. The Papacy's role as a moral and spiritual leader has also been a constant, providing guidance and inspiration to millions of believers across the centuries.

The legacy of the Papacy is one of profound impact—not only within the Catholic Church but also in the broader context of world history. Its contributions to theology, philosophy, art, and politics have left an indelible mark on human civilization. As we look to the future, the Papacy's ongoing commitment to addressing global challenges and fostering a message of hope and compassion will continue to shape its role in the world.

In conclusion, the history of the Papacy is a testament to the enduring power of faith, the importance of leadership, and the resilience of an institution that has stood the test of time. The Papacy's epic story is one of continuous evolution, reflecting the dynamic interplay between tradition and innovation, authority and service. As we move forward, the lessons of the past will continue to inform and inspire the Papacy's journey, ensuring its place as a central and enduring force in the spiritual and temporal realms.

Made in United States
Cleveland, OH
10 May 2025

16822619R00028